The Peak District:

PICTURES FROM THE PAST

LINDSEY PORTER

British Library Cataloguing in
Publication Data

Porter, Lindsey
   The Peak District.
   1. Peak District (England)—
   History
   2. Peak District (England)—
   Description and travel— Views
   I. Title
   942.5′11′0222   DA670.D4

For Stella

ISBN 0 86190 125 8

Printed in the UK by Billings of
Worcester for the publishers
Moorland Publishing Co Ltd, 9-11
Station Street, Ashbourne,
Derbyshire, DE6 1DE England.
Telephone: (0335) 44486

Contents

Acknowledgements

The author wishes to acknowledge his thanks to the
following sources for the use of their photographs.
Other photographs are from the author's collection.

Matlock Library: 1-6, 8-11, 14, 17-19, 21, 24-7, 30-1,
   37-8, 40, 48-9, 51-6, 60-1, 63, 70, 72, 79, 85, 91, 98,
   104, 107, 112-16, 140, 143, 161-2, 167, 170-2, 178,
   187, 189
Derby Library: 12-13, 15, 22, 28-9, 34, 39, 41, 43-5,
   50, 62, 71, 73-4, 78, 83, 88-90, 99, 103, 105, 108,
   110-11, 146-51, 153, 158-60, 163-4, 166, 168-9,
   173-4
Bolehill WI: 35-6, 96, 106, 129-30
Mrs L. Baggaley: 64-9
G. Ellis: 109, 123, 131, 175-6
Mr J. Alcock: 7, 82, 86, 102
L & GRP, courtesy of David & Charles Ltd: 124-7
J. Brocklebank: 84, 132-3, 135
Mrs H. Green: 57-8, 188
J.A. Fleming: 122, 128
Albion Galleries, Hanley: 47
D. Blackhurst: 119
Dr J. Hollick: 118
Mr & Mrs J. Coates: 100
Mr G. Coupe: 42

References to 'Pevsner' refer to Sir Nikolaus Pevsner's
Buildings of England Series, published on a county
basis by Penguin.

Introduction

Photographs present a unique opportunity of bringing history alive; they present a picture to illustrate the written word. Consequently a collection of photographs such as those gathered together here can illustrate our history as in a unique way. This is particularly useful when dealing with an area as well known and as popular as the Peak District.

It is not just buildings and the countryside which change; people change too. Our fashions and way of life change, as well as our attitudes to life and our environment. All of this is brought alive in this book. The changes in the landscape can be quite staggering. One has to think no further than the upper Derwent Valley which is now flooded behind three large dams. A photograph of Ashopton — but one taken much earlier than is generally seen — and the scene at Cox's bridge below Ashopton are included here. It is quite a pretty bridge really, but not one of great importance. However it does show the type of scene we can no longer witness. It is for this reason that I have included the statue at Osmaston Manor; a relic of an era which passed with the demolition of the house. It is not just the destruction of the landscape which is represented here, for there is the unique photograph of the construction of the Monsal Head Viaduct, dated 1861. It was a piece of civil engineering which caused considerable distress to many, including Ruskin, by the intrusion it made into the landscape. Its great size is now its saviour for maintenance costs are much lower than the cost of demolishing it.

As well as changes in the landscape, there are the changes in techniques caught by the camera, such as the wooden scaffolding poles used to build the Maynard Arms at Grindleford in 1908. Then there is behaviour of Victorian shopkeepers, of proudly displaying their wares on the street. Even Butcher Trafford at Leek put on an impressive display with many carcasses hanging from the front of the shop. One suspects, however, that this was an urban rather than a rural preoccupation for competition was less — or non-existent — in the villages.

Changes in our way of life are obviously reflected; the departure of the horse and cart in favour of the motor vehicle had a massive impact. We are no longer directly dependent upon steam whether for railways, stationary steam engines or traction engines. The mobility created by the motor car terminated the isolation of the Peak District, changing it from an entirely rural environment to a mixed environment, with the development as urban-sprawl and dormitory villages. The car also accentuated the area's popularity with visitors. The spa towns of Buxton and Matlock grew with the railway era but the car has increased the pressures of tourism to an extent previously unknown.

Our photographs reflect the graceful era enjoyed by the wealthy visitors to the spas who came 'to take the waters'. Today, their hydros are no more. Some, buildings survive in other guises, including one — the Haddon Grove Hydro in London Road — which has recently reverted to being a hotel. Some hydros have gone however, such as at Matlock Bath, as well as the huge Empire Hotel at Buxton.

Other visitors came to the dales to appreciate their beauty. The impact of these visitors was very little, either on the infrastructure of the community or on the dales themselves. One has only to think of the present degeneration of the paths in Beresford Dale to a virtual mud-bath and then compare it with the view reproduced in this book.

Perhaps one of the great charms of a collection of photographs such as this lies in the little changes which can be observed if one takes the trouble to examine the illustrations carefully: changes in fashion, villagers queuing at a travelling shop, where the vehicle has solid tyres. The view of the water barrel at Ilam reminds us of the days when many rural cottages lacked even the basic amentities we take for granted today.

In any work such as this, one can easily point to areas which have not been covered and to activities which have not been included. This is particularly true of agriculture. Here working techniques have changed considerably, but few photographs seem to record this.

One of the joys of putting together a collection of photographs is the discovery of bygone scenes which have a personal interest. In my case, the discovery of the photographs of Beresford Hall, the aqueduct piers in Lathkilldale, the view of Ilam Hall from the Italian garden, readily spring to mind. Another joy is the sheer delight of scenes such as the horse and cart outside Tufa Cottage in the Via Gellia. These are scenes which we shall not witness again. I do hope that they give you as much enjoyment as they have given me. The photographic collection of the Local History Sections of the Derbyshire County Library Service at Matlock and Derby have been used extensively and it is a reflection of the value of these collections that I have included so many. I hope that the publicity this book will give to the collections will result in an increase in donations of old photographs to these libraries.

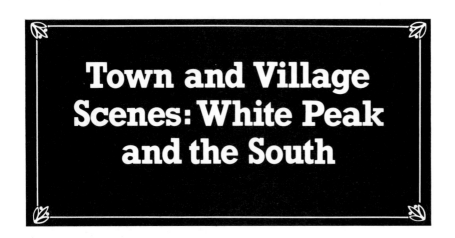
1-2 Bakewell developed as a crossing point of the River Wye in Anglo-Saxon times. The church has some Saxon fragments remaining although only a mound remains of its castle of about AD920. It became a market town in 1254 and still retains its cattle market. Here is Rutland Square in 1914 and 1923 showing the Rutland Hotel. The square was set out in 1824 by the Duke of Rutland in an urban renewal scheme designed to capture some of the 'spa status' of Buxton. The hotel dates from this time also. The two views reflect the change in emphasis from horse power to the motor car which occured at this time.

3 This is a further view of Rutland Square, Bakewell from Bridge Street, taken in 1914. The bank on the right dates from 1838. Note the boy with his hoop and the other boy with his push-chair.

1

676/6

4

4 This view of Bakewell looks back to where the previous photograph was taken. It is earlier however, having been taken in 1891. Note that the gas lamps do not exist now and that the low building (third from the left) has also gone.

5

5 Bridge Street, Bakewell, showing the Market Hall before it was renovated by the Peak District National Park Authority. It dates from the early seventeenth century. The white canopy reads "A. Cresswell and Son. Fruiterers and Caterers" but the older wooden sign reads "Central Refreshment Rooms. Cycling and Picnic Parties catered for Arthur Cresswell"

6 The street to the south of Rutland Square is Matlock Street, shown here. Some properties on the left have been demolished to give better access to the market and the more recent carpark.

7 This photograph of Bath Street, Bakewell, was taken in 1890 just before the new Town Hall was built on the site of this building.

8 The rise of the hydropathic industry in Matlock during the nineteenth century firmly established its development into a busy town. Here is Crown Square with its tram shelter (now removed to the adjacent gardens), a tram and many people going about their

business. The view over the bridge (behind the tram) shows that the photograph was taken before the bridge was widened in 1904. Notice the buildings on the left of the photograph in Crown Square, which have now been demolished.

9-10 Here are two views of Bank Road, Matlock, together with its tramway which operated from 1893 until 1927. The fare was 2d to ride up the hill, but only 1d to ride down! It had a gradient of 1 in 5½ and was the steepest cable

tramway in the world on a public road.

Flooding of Crown Square occured at regular intervals and here the tram creates a bow wave as it heads for the tramway shelter.

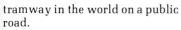

11 Matlock Bath has changed a great deal since this photograph was taken. The buildings on the right, which included the Royal Museum and Petrifying Well have gone. The well of course remains and 'petrified' items can be seen now as then. The view is from a few yards up river of the Pavilion. William Adam in his *Gem of the Peak* stated that the Royal Museum 'has been made into a museum about twenty-two years [about 1829], and contains a great variety of fine things in Derbyshire Spar, Marbles and Italian goods, which do great credit to the taste of the proprietor.....'

12-13 Matlock Bath railway station and the Midland Hotel taken from the Promenade by the river Derwent. Both this and the next scene were taken by Richard Keene of Derby, early in this century.

Just upstream from the station is the entrance to High Tor. It is from near here that the new cable cars start their journey across the valley to the Heights of Abraham. The main road between Matlock and Cromford has been widened, reducing the width of the gardens and also resulting in the demolition of many properties.

15 Topley Pike on the A6 in Ashford Dale, near Buxton. This tranquil spot has since changed! The trunk road has been widened and the area somewhat disfigured by quarrying operations. Today, the dog, standing patiently in the road, would be more wary of the frequently passing heavy traffic than curiosity at a box camera. The postcard is postmarked 1903.

14 The Opera House, Buxton, with the winter garden at the left-hand side. The Opera House was built in 1903 and has recently been refurbished. It was regularly used by well known operatic companies and held in high esteem, both for the quality of its decoration and performances. Once more it is the cultural centre of the district, serving the arts well, despite having only limited finance.

The indoor and heated garden has also been refurbished and was re-opened by Countess Spencer.

16 Cowlow Bridge and Topley Pike. The bridge has since been replaced and the signal and signal box have been removed. The area between the bridge and Topley Pike is now much more wooded, which screens the view of the Pike and the quarry.

16

17 The Square, Eyam, in 1919. Only the street scene has altered, the buildings, by and large, remaining the same. Notice the steam engine in the middle of the photograph.

18 These buildings opposite Eyam Church, also photographed in 1919, have also hardly changed. In fact the main alterations would appear to be a change of use of the shop to a house and the reduction in height of the two large chimneys at the end of the street. The building with the flag pole is now the National Westminster Bank. The public house is the Bulls Head, originally the Talbot Inn. Apparently it was so called as early as 1606 and changed to its current name about 1710.

18

19 Eyam Hall and the village stocks, also taken in 1919. The wooden boards of the stocks have been renewed recently. The Hall dates from the late seventeenth century, apparently built between 1672 and 1676. The great plague, which killed 257 inhabitants of the village in 1655-6, had been sufficiently forgotten about for substantial rebuilding and investment to take place.

20-21 Two views of Shining Cliff at the junction of Eyam Dale and Middleton Dale. The earlier view is undated, but the properties had obviously been redeveloped as the Ball Inn by the time the second photograph had been taken in 1919. Merlin's Cavern, a small lead mine-cum-cave a short way up Eyam Dale, was opened as a show cave for a short period at the end of the nineteenth century. Middleton Dale was quite an industrial area in the nineteenth century with two lead mining cupolas or smelting mills, limestone quarrying and limekilns, plus the Watergrove lead mine with its substantial chimney at the head of the dale. The site of the buildings is now a car park for the quarry opposite.

22 The western end of Stoney Middleton Village. The brook down-stream of the boys has now been culverted and the buildings adjacent to the men have been demolished. It is, however, possible to identify the remaining buildings. Today, this is a busy trunk road, not the quiet rural scene shown here. The building in the middle of the photograph is the Lover's Leap Cafe. This may have been the 'small inn' refered to by William Adam in 1851 in his *Gem of the Peak*. He also states 'From the summit of this fearful precipice [Lover's Leap], about the year 1760, a love-stricken damsel of the name of Baddeley, threw herself down, and strange as it may appear, she sustained but little injury; however, it had a salutary effect on her mind, and she became serious, and lived much respected for many years afterwards'. Obviously Adam did not consider her suicide attempt to be 'serious'.

23 The Kings Head in Commercial Road, Tideswell. It was situated opposite the Bulls Head and was on the grassy area adjacent to the Co-op and the entrance to the church. The road has also been widened. The pub sold Tennant's ales and stouts and the licensee was Thomas Needham.

24-25 Millers Dale. Sometimes changes in the landscape are of only subtle effect, as in these two views of Millers Dale. The quarry, which had four limekilns above the railway bridge, has closed and the road up to it, although still remaining has lost its scarring effect on the hillside under a mantle of grass. Note also the cab between the buildings and in front of a tearoom at the side of the Railway Hotel. In the second photograph, the building on the right hand side is the old mill; it has now gone but its waterwheel remains. The card is dated 1903.

26-27 Sheepwash Bridge at Ashford showing the celebrated sheepwash on the left-hand side. This bridge, with two more in Ashford, were crossing points over the River Wye for packhorse trains. Ashford itself had a fort (Ashford Castle) and a lead smelter is recorded here in the Domesday Book. It was also here that the prehistoric Portway forded the river and one of the village bridges is still known as Fillyford Bridge. The second feature is of the old pump in the village.

28

29

30

28 This old Puritan chapel in Ashford apparently remained empty for some years until it was converted into a YMCA which opened in May 1907. The caption accompanying this photograph records that 'Nordault lies buried under the floor'. This photograph is thought to have been taken in 1907. The chapel was built by William Newton, the 'Apostle of the Peak'. It was used by the YMCA as a 'youth club'.

29 A watermill at Rowsley, on the River Wye.

30 The caption to this photograph reads 'Oker Hill, Matlock, showing view of famous Oker Tree immortalised by the Poet Wordsworth'. This particular sonnet is quoted in full in Adam's *Gem of the Peak* on page 93. It describes the meeting on the hill of two brothers, each planting a tree before parting forever.

31 Two Dales, near Matlock, showing a group of people outside the Plough Inn.
This delightful village is now very much a commuter village, but the centre still retains its character. The village was the scene of the discovery of a Anglo-Saxon cross shaft of eleventh-century age. It was removed to Bakewell where it may be seen, re-erected in the churchyard at the east end of the church.

32 Hartington market place in 1895. Not a lot has altered but the feeling of a great expanse as shown here seems to have been lost with the creation of pavements and a central car park. The stable block facing the photographer has been replaced by a garage block, now converted into a sheepskin and craft shop. It is a pity this photograph was not taken 3 years earlier, when the two-storey house behind the horse and cart was built. It would have been nice to have seen the previous building here too!

33 This is the site of Ecton Copper Mines in the Manifold Valley. The building on the far left was the home of the mine manager when the mine was operating. The building left of centre has now been demolished but was the 'clockhouse' smelter. It was built in the late eighteenth century and was so called because it has a round stone faced clock on the far side. The old chapel was built by the Leek and Manifold Valley Light Railway and was the foreman's hut, presumably to supervise the extraction of the old tips which were purchased by the railway from the Duke of Devonshire at ³⁄₄d per ton. After completion of the line in 1904, Sir Thomas Wardle of nearby Swainsley Hall, bought it and turned it into a chapel where he played the organ. The Wetton vicar officiated, but services stopped when Sir Thomas died in 1910. The building was later moved to a farm on the south side of Wetton village.

34 The Druids Inn near Birchover, photographed in April 1912. It was built shortly before 1846 and in the grounds are the Rowtor Rocks. The premises have now been substantially extended.

35 This horse and cart was photographed at the foot of the Green in Bolehill near Wirksworth.

36 The Railway Inn (now a farmhouse) at the corner of Oakerthorpe Road and Steeple Grange, Bolehill, near Wirksworth. The men are (from left) George Robinson, the lessee of Black Rocks Quarry; Robert Limb his foreman and John Housley in the milk float.

37 Tufa Cottage in the Via Gellia, photographed in 1891. The road was built by Philip Gell, of Hopton Hall, in 1791-2. It was used to ease transportation between his lead mines and Cromford, where there was a smelter (on the site of Cromford Church) and of course, the Cromford Canal. The road was turnpiked in 1804. Today the tranquility of this dale has been lost for the road is one of the few lorry routes across the district.

38 Towards the Cromford end of the Via Gellia is the road to Bonsall and the Pig of Lead public house, shown here. The name is a reminder of the lead mining

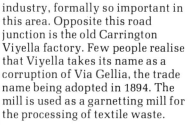

industry, formally so important in this area. Opposite this road junction is the old Carrington Viyella factory. Few people realise that Viyella takes its name as a corruption of Via Gellia, the trade name being adopted in 1894. The mill is used as a garnetting mill for the processing of textile waste.

39 This cottage stood in the Via Gellia at the T-junction where the roads to Middleton-by-Wirksworth and Hopton leave the valley at Rider Point. The cottage, along with the building adjacent to the horse and the garden to the right of the finger post have all disappeared during road improvements.

40 Coldwell Street, Wirksworth,
with the Gilkin in the distance.
Wirksworth still 'dresses its wells'
although they have all now
disappeared. Coldwell Street has
some fine property worth looking
at, including The Manor House,
behind the gate on the left of the
photograph and the old manse,
which faces the Manor House.
There are several fine properties in
Wirksworth, which has an
important conservation area. It
also has a round churchyard,
indicative of an early christian site
and one of the best examples in the
country of a Saxon carved stone
coffin lid.

41 This is the original Crich Stand after it had been struck by lightning in 1901. It was built in 1851 at a cost of £210. The lightning also split the masonry and this forced its closure as a viewing platform. After World War I, it was demolished and rebuilt further back from the quarry edge. It was dedicated as a memorial to the Sherwood Foresters who fell in the war.

Cliff Quarry dates from the 1840s and was connected by an inclined tramway to limekilns at Ambergate. It was owned by George Stephenson, the railway surveyor and engineer. The quarry closed in 1957 and in 1959 the locomotive sheds and other buildings were taken over by the Tramway Museum.

42 A corner in Tissington Village.

43   The photograph of Parwich
Church was taken in about 1870
just before the church was entirely
rebuilt. The glass in the windows
appears to be broken. The flight of
steps rising to first floor level were
used by the musicians and choir to
reach the gallery. It is not very
often that previous church
buildings are recorded on
photographs, but the
redevelopment of the church came
much later than most Victorian
restoration schemes.

44 This cross in Ilam village was erected in memory of Mary Watts Russell in 1840; it added a fine centre piece for the new model village. Few people who see the cross nowadays appreciate that it used to be a fountain, with the water flowing out into six troughs. Whether this was intended for domestic as well as horse consumption is not too clear. However, this photograph shows a water barrel next to the boy. The top of the cross was displaced in 1962 by severe gales. It is a pity that it was found expedient to replace it with a simple stone cross, rather than a faithfully reproduced replica of the original.

45 This is a view of Ilam Village from Bunster Hill. It is a fascinating photograph and somewhat surprising that such a view is rare. One would have thought that it would have been very popular with photographers.

In the distance of course, is Ilam Hall. To the right is the school and school house. Immediately behind the school is the entrance to the hall for domestic staff who were not allowed to use the main drive. Notice also the road to the church from St Bertram's bridge which has also become disused and overgrown. The three hayricks represent a past practice now seldom seen.

46 Consall Forge in the Churnet
Valley situated between
Cheddleton and Froghall. In the
foreground is the old public road.
As a result of a landslip, this was
closed by the County Council and
access today is only via a private
estate road. The cottages on the left
have been demolished and the
white painted cottage is now owned
by the Caldon Canal Society. Just
off to the right is the Black Lion Inn.
The canal is just below the cottage,
but is not visible in this
photograph. Consall Forge takes its
name from an old iron forge
established prior to 1655.

46

47 Ipstones, near Leek, showing the village post office and schools. Ipstones grew as a mining village, exploiting local reserves of ironstone and coal. In 1861, the census revealed that the 122 native male workers had been swelled by 177 immigrant workers. It is situated astride the turnpike road from Cheadle to Butterton Moor End and the village toll house still survives. The authorisation of the turnpike was in 1770.

48

49

48-50 Here are three views taken in Ashbourne, showing Ashbourne Hall, when it was in use as the Ashbourne Hall Hotel; Church Street and St John's Street. The hall has been partly demolished and the remaining part used as a library, but the street buildings are very largely as now. Gone are the horses and carts, gas lamps and empty streets. The buildings reflect the street layout established in the thirteenth century when the town was redeveloped away from the area of the church, which was more susceptible to flooding.

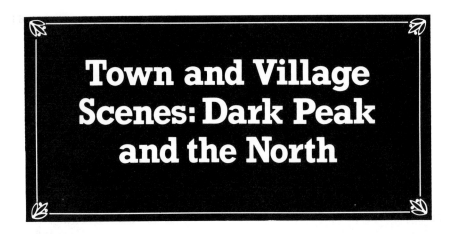

Town and Village Scenes: Dark Peak and the North

51

51-4 Castleton developed over the centuries as a mining village, with lead mines on the adjacent limestone. It had been important from early times of course, with its Norman Castle overlooking the valley. As a sideline, so to speak, rope making was established in the entrance to Peak Cavern and Blue John stone was exploited at the Blue John Mine near to Mam Tor.

Here are four views showing Cross Street in 1921; the market place in 1909 including the building occupied by the Old Barn Craft Shop; Church Street and the George Hotel in 1909; a corner of the village with the Brooklyn tea room.

52

55 Down the valley from
Castleton, the next village is Hope,
situated on the cross roads of two
ancient highways and also close to
the Roman fort of Brough. This and
the following five photographs
show a selection of scenes around
the village. Here we have the Old
Hall Hotel and the smithy beyond.
The small building is the site of
The Hope Chest.

56 The former Blacksmiths Arms
and Post Office. These are now
houses with a shop at the left-hand
end. The buildings on the far left
have been demolished and the site
is currently occupied by an unused
petrol filling station. These
buildings are to the left of the
Hope Chest.

57 School children at play in the main street.

58 Children at play outside the Old Hall Hotel

59

60

59 Brough Mill. This scene has altered significantly although the buildings are easily identified. The old corn mill is now occupied by William Eyre and Sons, agricultural merchants. The mill building was extended out to the right in 1984. The frontage of these buildings now extends out into the roadway. The horse has just come over the bridge, which was built in 1824. A Roman fort called *Navio* existed at Brough. It was occupied for nearly four centuries and there appears to have been a large settlement or *vicus*, adjacent to the fort.

60 The George Hotel at Hathersage in 1919. This is the view up the Sheffield road and the view down it is shown in the next photograph. The building to the right of the inn sign has since been redeveloped and is now William and Glyn's Bank. Today, the motorist would find this trunk road heavily congested and not as empty as in 1919!

61 The Hotel is now The Hathersage Inn and the building below it is now the National Westminster Bank. It is of interesting appearance but was unfortunately overlooked by Pevsner. Not a great deal else has changed, except that the telegraph poles and gas lamps have gone.

62 The George Hotel prior to the redevelopment seen in the photograph above. The high pitched roof on the skyline is now the building occupied by the Youth Hostel.

62

63 Surprise View on Millstone
Edge, photographed in 1919, with a
charabanc heading for Hathersage.
In reality, the nearest vehicle has
been added to the photograph,
which is why it appears to be on a
collision course!

64 This photograph of
Grindleford Bridge from where the
road turns up to Hathersage was
taken around 1888. The house on
the right was formerly the Bell Inn
and hostelry. It was converted into
two houses around 1880 and is one
of the oldest houses in the village.
The road has since been widened
and half of the building has been
demolished. It now stands quite a

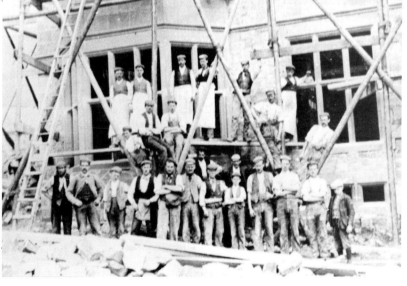

way below road level. The land down to the bridge has now been developed, obscuring the view of the bridge.

65 The building of the Maynard Arms Hotel in Grindleford, about 1908. It was called the Maynard Arms because it was built on land owned by the Maynard family. Notice the wooden scaffold poles.

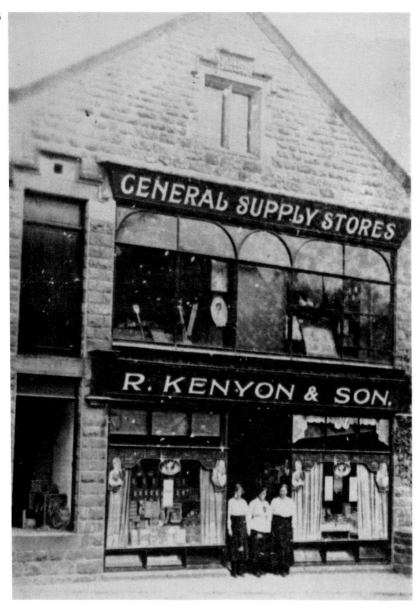

66 Grindleford General Store built around 1914 by either Robert or Peter Kenyon. It was a very fine shop for a small village with excellent living accommodation. After prospering for a while, the firm became bankrupt and the shop was used for various purposes; a bakers and also a café amongst other things. It was situated next to the Sir William Hotel and was eventually bought by the brewery. In 1972 it was demolished and the land made into a car-park to serve the hotel. The three ladies in the photograph are Peter Kenyon's daughters.

67 Grindleford General Store and Post Office near the village green in the 1880s. The wooden building was part of the premises and there was very little else around in this part of the village. The buildings, which have since been altered, are situated almost opposite the Sir William Hotel on the corner of Sir William Hill.

68 This is a close up of the Village Store and Post Office seen in the previous photograph. It was run by Miss Rebecca Kenyon. When she retired in 1903, the Post Office changed to the ownership of Mr T.A. Morton who brought it down onto the main road where the butchers shop is now. The house on the right was taken down in 1958 for road widening.

69 Grindleford Railway Station taken shortly after it opened in 1898. It shows Mr Kenyon's horse buses awaiting passengers for Grindleford, Calver, Baslow, Stoney Middleton, as well as Eyam and Foolow.

70 The Chequers Inn on Froggatt Edge. This is still a roadside inn, and the adjacent buildings have been incorporated into the pub. The buildings on the right of the photograph have now gone and the site is now a car park.

70

71 The Fox House Inn on the Sheffield Road from Hathersage.

72 This photograph is endorsed Mrs Elliott's Cottage, Baslow. Internal photographs in cottages are not that common and this shows the typical rangegrate, paraffin lamps and kettle on the fire.

73 Ashopton village before it was demolished and the area inundated to form Ladybower reservoir. In fact it must be an early photograph of the village because the building on the left is the Ashopton Inn, and photographs taken early this century show that other buildings were added on in part of the garden to the right of the inn. The inn was built in 1824 and demolished in January 1943. Compare closely this photograph with picture 35 in *Bygone Days in the Peak District.*

73

74 This is Cox's Bridge and the confluence of the rivers Ashop and Derwent. The Derwent is on the left and under the bridge, the Ashop being on the right.

75-7 The scene in the Market Place of Chapel-en-le-Frith has altered significantly in some ways. The road has been widened and the light coloured building behind the cows has been demolished. The photograph was taken before a water trough was placed for the animals in 1897. The Pack Horse Inn on the left is now the Royal Oak but the Kings Arms Hotel at the top of the Market Place has retained its name. Two contemporary photographs showing the interior of the hotel are included.

78 Lower Lane in Chinley. Like
many rural villages, it has now lost
its co-op. This was run by the New
Mills Co-operative Society Limited.
The other buildings have not
altered significantly.

79 Goyts Bridge over the Wildmoorstone Brook in the upper Goyt Valley, photographed in 1891. It was situated on an old saltway to Buxton. When the area was flooded by the Errwood Reservoir in the 1960s the bridge was rebuilt upstream. The old packhorse route came by way of Jenkin Chapel (where there is a Saltersford Hall), and Pym Chair. It left the valley for the top of Long Hill and the descent into Buxton.

At Work

80

80 Sharpening a scythe at Longnor. This is Mr Thomas Smith, who had a small holding at nearby Carder Green. He apparently died in 1926 which would seem to date this photograph to fifty to sixty years ago. Although it would appear that this photograph was taken at his garden, the scythe was an indispensable tool, especially during haymaking. They still have a use on some farms for cutting down thistles, nettles etc.

81 J.M. Nuttall's cheese factory at Hartington. It dates from the early 1870s when it started with an initial milk intake of fifty gallons per day and pigs were kept as a sideline to eat the whey. It probably made Derby cheese at this time. After being unused from 1894 to 1900, it was aquired by J.M. Nuttall who commenced making stilton cheese. A fire in 1929 destroyed the factory which was only of wood and iron construction. In 1962 it was purchased by the Milk Marketing Board, who still use the Nuttall trade mark.

82 Although the original photograph is not of good quality, it does show reasonably well the process of sheep dipping at Bakewell, near to Holme Bridge. This was often a wet and thankless task and few photographs survive showing the work in process in the rivers of the Peak District.

83 This early photograph shows a farmer with his horse and cart at the entrance to Grindsbrook Clough, at the rear of Edale Village.

84 This is Bretton Clough Farm. It was originally two houses, the left-hand one being Hawley's Farm and the lower, right-hand one being Fairest Clough House, which had a datestone of 1782. It was last occupied in 1919 and the roof was removed in 1935. The last occupant was Joseph Townsend who was quoted as saying he had 'two houses and over 100 ackers o'land for forty pun a year rent, an' it were as dear as hell fire at that'. Running a farm on the poor quality soils of the Peak District hills still remains a hard and not very lucrative occupation.

85 The Smithy at Hope in 1932. It has since been demolished.

86

86 This is Bakewell smithy. Indoor photographs of workshops such as this give a good insight into working conditions, tools of the trade and way of life of small businesses.

87 Mr Sam Sykes the village cobbler at Longnor in his workshop. A careful look at the picture reveals such detail as the lockable drawer in his seat, the glue pot on the shelf, etc.

87

88 One of the last of the Belper nailmakers. The manufacture of nails in the town goes back to at least 1313, when it was first recorded, but it died out in the nineteenth century. Nailers' shops can still be seen around the town, such as in Joseph Street.

89 Another Belper industry was crate making and this photograph was taken around 1890. The crates seem to be more intricate than those manufactured in North Staffordshire for the pottery industry. The town's textile mills must have created quite a demand for the crates.

90-1 Peak Cavern in Castleton. This interior view was taken in 1896. Note the ropes during the course of manufacture in the cave. The last ropemaker ceased work only a few years ago. Originally the rope makers lived in little cottages built within the mouth of the cave.

92 W. Barnes were ironmongers in the Market Place, Ashbourne. They occupied the premises where Damar now trade. Here is their delivery cart out on its rounds. See also No. 104.

93 Traffords were well respected family butchers, occupying premises at the bottom of the

Market Place in Leek. They obviously favoured the Victorian preoccupation of hanging what often seems to be the whole stock of the business on the outside of the shop. Traffords also has a delivery cart which features in this photograph. The business closed in the 1960s.

94

95

94 A carrier in Longnor. The two shops behind the horse are a grocers and a corndealers. Off the picture to the left was the village smithy and the Market Place.

95 In the nineteenth century, the Churnet Valley saw a considerable exploitation of iron ore, between Cheddleton and Froghall. The mines were situated on the valley sides and in the fields above, but the red-coloured ore was brought down to the Caldon Canal for shipment. This tramway bridge brought waggons over the river, railway and canal. It existed from around 1860 to 1887 and was built approximately where the footbridge is now, on the upstream side of Podmore's flint mill, below Consal Forge.

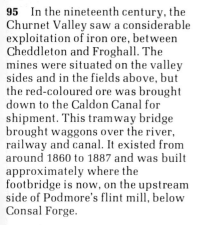

96 Lead mines are scattered throughout the Peak District and it was a practice to secure the top of abandoned shafts with a stone 'beehive'. This one is on the Bage Mine at Bolehill, near Wirksworth and was photographed about sixty years ago. The building behind the shaft is a mine building and they were known as a 'coe'. Quite often the shaft was under its roof. This not only kept the mine secure but kept out the weather too.

97 The loss of the Watergrove Lead Mine chimney in 1960 was a principle reason for the formation of the Peak District Mines Historical Society which now runs the Mining Museum at Matlock Bath. The chimney was built in 1837 and was eighty feet high. Watergrove Mine was situated at the top of Middleton Dale on the road to Warolow Mires.

98

98 Lead mining was the staple industry of the Peak for centuries, along with agriculture. Earlier this century, Mill Close Mine at Darley Dale was the biggest lead mine in the country and this undated photograph shows a group of the miners behind the ore tubs. After a long and varied history the mine, beset by water problems and dwindling reserves of ore, closed in 1939-40.

99 This is a fascinating photograph. It is possibly the only one to survive which shows the old aqueduct piers in Lathkilldale at their full height. They were built to support a launder which carried a leat from the southern (left-hand) bank to the northern (right-hand) bank. The water supply was to a 35-feet diameter waterwheel at the Mandale Mine, where the ruined engine house still survives. The aqueduct was built in 1840 but the mine closed in 1851. The waterwheel pit survives behind the engine house. The bases of the piers survive, some being around ten feet high, but their original height can be gauged from the line of the leat on each side of the valley. This would appear to be another Richard Keene photograph with the photographer also admiring the view.

99

100 Apes Tor Quarry, Ecton in the Manifold Valley, showing the separator, driven by a steam engine. The quarry was worked earlier this century. It is well known for the contorted strata revealed by quarrying operations.

101 This scene was taken at Froghall in the Churnet Valley. The buildings stood adjacent to the Navigation Inn but all the buildings, including the Inn, have been recently demolished. The canal workers are hauling a maintenance boat and presumably were employed by the North Staffordshire Railway Company who owned the canal. Man power was only generally used when boats were required to be moved a short distance. The alternative would have been to fetch a horse from one of the stables at Froghall wharf.

102

102 This was Bakewell Post Office prior to 1894. Notice the mailcart, which has arrived from Chesterfield. At the time that this photograph was taken, a Miss Swain was the postmistress and she is seen standing by the door.

103 This is a fascinating photograph capturing a bygone era. The shirehorses are hauling timber over the River Dove at Ellastone. The horses are just about to negotiate a tight bend which is why they are ranging right over to the far side of the highway. This old photograph is undated.

103

104 The days of retailing of agricultural machinery by town centre shops have now gone, although in some cases only recently. It was possible to see machinery, on the pavement outside Marsden's shop in the Market Place, Wirksworth until 1983. On the right of the photograph is the shop of Wooddise and Desborough who advertised themselves as Agricultural Implement Makers and Dealers. The shops on the left of the picture are Elkes' Dining Rooms and the Ashbourne Coffee House, now Spencer's Restaurant. Barnes were ironmongers in Ashbourne's Market Place and their cart also features on picture No. 92.

105 Carter's Mill, at the foot of Haddon Grove in Lathkilldale. The site of this corn mill is now just a ruin, but it is possible to see where the wheel pit was and two mill stones remain, along with the weir. The mill was built in the early nineteenth century and it survived, although disused, until World War II when the wheel was scrapped.

106

107

106 The remains of Mr Henry Flint's brick kiln which used to exist by the side of the Cromford and High Peak Railway at Flint's Wharf. This photograph was taken about sixty years ago.

108 The scene at the top of the incline is shown here in this photograph taken before Crich Stand was rebuilt after World War I. The view shows what is now the site of the Tramway Museum and appears to have been taken from the road from Crich to Lea. The building in the middle of the photograph still survives, overshadowed by the tramsheds. The waggons are stone waggons, used for transporting the limestone to Ambergate.

107 The Ambergate limekilns photographed between 1908 and 1923. The kilns were originally operated by George Stephenson and burnt limestone brought down the incline from Crich. There were a total of twenty kilns, giving an output capacity of 50,000 tons per annum. The limeworks closed on 2 October 1965. The incline from Crich is visible in the right background, behind the kilns.

109 This scene of great activity shows the early days of the construction of the Ladybower reservoir. Across the right of the photograph can be seen the deep trench which was filled with concrete to give additional strength to the dam wall. The dam was opened in 1945 by King George VI. The villages of Derwent and Ashopton were demolished and inundated.

110

110 The thermal baths at the Crescent at Buxton also had what was termed a mineral or mud bath. It involved the immersion of the patient in a bath of the thermal water and peat cut from the Axe Edge Moors. Here are nine men cutting the peat in winter, ready for the new season. The mineral baths were also known as the Moor Baths.

111 This photograph shows another unusual occupation. Some Monyash men were employed in successive seasons at the beginning of the century to literally undertake the 'spadework' for excavations being undertaken at Arbor Low stone circle. This photograph was taken during 1901 and another survives of the 1902 season. Third from the left is Mr Charles Millington who had the distinction of being the last of the 'old men', as the Peak District's miners were known. The term was also used for the mine workings themselves, particularly when miners broke into worked-out and abandoned lead veins.

112 This fine cart built for G. Else of Matlock was the last cart built by the Matlock firm of Greatorex and Sons. It was photographed upon completion in 1922.

113

114

113 Matlock Bridge dates from the thirteenth century although it has been rebuilt several times. Here we see the bridge being widened in 1903-4. Notice the track laid for the steam crane, running across the front of the arches.

115 This photograph is captioned 'Matlock Bath from Harp Edge'. However, its particular interest is that it shows Masson Mill, built by Sir Richard Arkwright, before the addition of the more modern buildings in the foreground, between the road and the river. The main buildings shown here were built in 1793. Frederick Arkwright sold the premises to the English Sewing Cotton Company in 1898. The latter extended the premises soon afterwards and it is probable that this photograph was taken before then. The cottages at the roadside opposite the mill have been demolished.

114 The River Derwent and High Tor. What is particularly interesting however, is the small works at the side of the road. It appears to be a wagon works and a mill stone can also be seen. The site has now been cleared and the road widened.

Steam and Steam Traction

116

116-17 The development by the Midland Railway of a rail link across the Peak between Rowsley and Buxton aroused considerable opposition. Indeed, it must have created a considerable scar, particularly in the section from Monsal Dale to Ashford Dale. Today, it blends into the landscape quite well and the Monsal Head viaduct which Ruskin hated is now one of the area's attractions.

Here are two views of it. The first is a remarkable photograph for it shows the bridge actually being built in 1861. The second shows a coal train about to cross the bridge.

117

118 This remarkable photograph shows workmen engaged in the construction of the railway tunnel on the Manifold Valley Light Railway at Swainsley. The locomotive is 0-4-2T *Skylark*, built in 1902 by Kerr Stuart and Co Ltd of Stoke-on-Trent. It eventually ended its days on the Snailbeach District Railway in Shropshire, where it was eventually scrapped in May 1950.

119 The Manifold Valley Light Railway only lasted for thirty years and here is the demolition train at Redhurst Crossing in 1934. Note the six-inch high platform and the old goods wagon which was used as a shelter. The open wagon is of standard gauge, being carried on the Light Railway's special thirty-inch transporter.

120-1 Two steam buses of the North Staffordshire Railway Company. The company operated a combined bus and rail operation. They were built by Strakers of Bristol and operated from 1904. The first photograph shows the bus boarding passengers at Leek for Waterhouses to connect with the Manifold Valley Light Railway. It also shows Leek Station in the background. The second photograph shows the Ashbourne to Waterhouses bus appropriately situated on the LNWR railway bridge in Church Street, Ashbourne. The fare from Leek to Waterhouses was 8d (eight old pence) and the buses held twenty-two passengers. It took an hour to travel the eight miles to Watehouses from either town.

LEEK, WATERHOUSES & HULME END.

122 Millers Dale was an important station because of its volume of limestone traffic. It was also an exchange station for traffic to Buxton which was off the through route. The locomotive is an ex-Midland Railway 0-6-0 No 58224, built in 1883. This photograph was taken in September 1955 shortly before the engine was withdrawn.

123

124

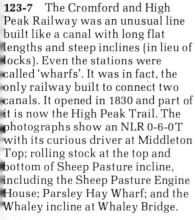

123-7 The Cromford and High Peak Railway was an unusual line built like a canal with long flat lengths and steep inclines (in lieu of locks). Even the stations were called 'wharfs'. It was in fact, the only railway built to connect two canals. It opened in 1830 and part of it is now the High Peak Trail. The photographs show an NLR 0-6-0T with its curious driver at Middleton Top; rolling stock at the top and bottom of Sheep Pasture incline, including the Sheep Pasture Engine House; Parsley Hay Wharf; and the Whaley incline at Whaley Bridge.

128

128   The former Ashbourne
Station in June 1956. The
locomotive is a former LNWR 0-8-0,
No 49210 class G1, built in 1913
and withdrawn in 1961. The station
was opened in 1852 and closed in
1963. The site has now been cleared
and used for a swimming pool and
car park.

129-30   This accident happened on
the Hopton incline of the Cromford
and High Peak Railway on 14
October 1937, when ex-NLR 0-6-0T
No 27521 was derailed with its four
wagons (loaded with limestone)
and a brake-van. The accident
happened on the curve at the
bottom of the incline and the driver
was killed. The engine was built in
1892 and rebuilt in 1910. It was,
however, scrapped following the
accident.

131 A goods train approaches Hindlow Station near Buxton. The background is Beswick's Lime Works, now Steetley's Quarry. The line is now single track and the station has been demolished. The photograph was taken around forty years ago.

132-3 The *Spar Queen*. This small narrow gauge locomotive hauled fluorspar from Eyam Edge to Waterfall Farm, near Foolow during World War I. The tonnage of spar

extracted from the dumps of old lead mines was immense. Mr William Robinson extracted 150,000 tons from around Miners Engine Mine and Broadlow Mine alone. Much of this was exported to the USA, hence the significance of 'Liverpool and Grindleford' on the side of the engine.

Steam wagons were also used to transport the spar and the second photograph shows one such wagon plus an early petrol driven lorry.

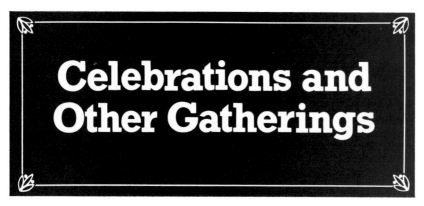

Celebrations and Other Gatherings

134 This must rank as one of the most unusual photographs taken at a gathering in the Peak. In fact, it presumably was taken for propaganda reasons. It shows infantry in Tideswell, recruiting volunteers for the relief of Mafeking in 1900. It was taken outside the now demolished Kings Head next door to the church. I wonder how many accepted the Queen's shilling.

134

135 This gathering is at Stoney Middleton, where a play is in progress.

136 Here some of the inhabitants of Sparrowpit gather with three carts on Peace Day 1918. Both of the cottages on the photograph survive. The one on the left is the Wanted Inn and the road to the right is the A623.

137 This scene of the Hartington militia is most interesting. It was taken between 1892 and 1894. The tall building in the right background is held locally to have been an old cotton mill, later in use as a penny lodging house when this photograph was taken. The cotton mill was built in 1776 by Thomas Cantrell and burnt down in 1786. In 1783 it was employing sixty people but little else is known. Facing it were built some workers' cottages which still survive with a plaque 'T & J C 1777'.

138 This illustration is endorsed 'Rutland (Bakewell) Habitation PL 1891'. It is presumably of the Primrose League and was taken outside Bridge House, Bakewell.

139 An open meeting of Primitive Methodists at Jimmy's Yard, Oakamoor in the Churnet Valley, taken at about the turn of the century. The speaker stands in an open railway wagon.

140 A maypole dance at
Middleton. Its a pity that the
maypole seems to have gone out of
favour at gatherings these days.

141 Queen Victoria's diamond jubilee celebrations at Leek in 1897. Note the uniforms of the policemen walking behind their band. A careful look reveals some interesting displays of late Victorian fashion. The photograph is taken in St Edwards Street.

142 A meeting of The Sea Lion and The Bear! This travelling bear performs outside the Sea Lion pub in Russell Street, Leek. Another illustration of a bear in the town survives and it appears that it must have performed in different parts of the town as a source of income for its owner.

143

144

143 These children have gathered
for the Coronation Celebrations for
George V in June 1911. The
photograph was taken in
Starkholmes village near to
Matlock.

144 A gathering in Eyam for the
annual sheeproast, with what looks
like oatcakes on the table.

145 The travelling shop in the
market place at Longnor. The
photograph is taken outside the
Horseshoe Inn, adjacent to the
market place.

The Good Life

146

146-8 These fascinating photographs of Beresford Hall near Hartington, once the home of Charles Cotton, are probably the only ones to survive. They were taken in 1857. One is described as 'The ruins of the West Wing'. In reality it was the intention of Mr Beresford-Hope, the owner to rebuild the house. However a shortage of funds stopped this. He rebuilt Sheen Church and one to the same design in Maidstone, where he lived. After lying empty for years, the hall eventually became derelict and was demolished, perhaps as late as the 1880s. In the grounds there survive a prospect tower, possibly some 300 years old, and Charles Cotton's fishing house. It originally had a bowling green in front of it plus these huge trees which have subsequently been removed.

149 Ilam Hall must have been the centre of an enchanting estate. It was set above weirs that made the river Manifold into a broad expanse of water, and with woodlands set out with numerous paths. Its lands stretched almost the length of Dovedale. The house was rebuilt in the 1820s in Tudor Gothic style by Jesse Watts-Russell. The view is most unusual. It shows the formal rooms from the Italian Garden. The latter still survives but the formal rooms were demolished fifty years ago and only the entrance hall and servants quarters survive.

The church is now obscured from this position by a line of trees which were planted about eighty years ago on the edge of the churchyard.

150-3 Osmaston Manor, near Ashbourne, was built as a mock Tudor mansion between 1846 and 1849 for Francis Wright, head of the Butterly Company. It was demolished in 1966. Wright built a railway in the cellar to carry coal to a hydraulic lift that lifted it up the four floors of the house. There were not many chimneys as such; most of the smoke was ducted away to a smoke tower which still survives.

Here we see the house, plus the smoke room and conservatory. Although the detail is very faint on the original, the window in the conservatory seems to contain the statue 'The Dawn of Love' shown in the other photograph included here.

THE DAWN OF LOVE

CALWICH ABBEY. 2053.

154-5 The south-west corner of the Peak District has lost a significant number of old mansions. Beresford Hall and Ilam Hall mentioned previously are just two examples. Here are two more, Calwich Abbey, built in 1849-50 and Wootton Hall, which was owned by the Bromley-Davenports of Capesthorne Hall. The entrance gates to Wootton Hall were re-erected in the garden of Capesthorne Hall.

156 The Earl of Shrewsbury lavished a huge fortune upon his home, Alton Towers and its immense garden. Following its sale seventy years ago, the grounds were stripped of much of their finery. Here we see the conservatory. above the arches where visitors could sit as an alterantive to the smaller alcove on the right known as 'le Refuge'. Note the ten statues, now gone, and the plant-laden urns beneath the arches. The whole scene helps to give us a good impression of the granduer that was Alton. Because of tree and bush growth, you can no longer view all on this photograph from this spot.

157 Chatsworth House viewed from the terrace. The bushes between the statues are much higher now of course, and now tend to obscure the view of the house, but there is little else which has changed. It is interesting to compare the bushes here with their size today and note how small they still are for sixty to seventy years' growth.

158 The former French Gardens at Chatsworth in front of the camelia house known as the 'First Duke's Greenhouse'. Several of the columns have now gone and this view is obstructed by a high yew hedge which has been planted between the columns. The four columns with the white statues remain but much of the other detail has gone, including the central feature with its carving. The area is now a rose garden.

159 The Great Conservatory at Chatsworth, photographed around 1872, some thirty or so years after its construction. It was designed by Joseph Paxton and was 277ft long, 123ft wide and 67ft high. It cost over £30,000, took eight boilers to heat it and incorporated seven miles of iron piping. When Queen Victoria visited it in 1843, it was lit by 12,000 lamps. The doorways were wide enough to take a carriage, and a carriageway was constructed down its length. It eventually became uneconomical to heat and was demolished around sixty-five years ago. The site is now occupied by a maze. This period of greenhouse building gave Paxton the experience he used to build the Crystal Palace for the Great Exhibtion of 1851.

157

160   This interesting photograph of the Great Hall at Haddon Hall dates from about 1876. The roof was replaced in 1923-5, otherwise everything dates from before 1500 and the structure itself dates from around 1370. Pevsner describes the screen (which dates from about 1450) as one of the best early hall screens in the country.

161-2   Thornbridge Hall, near Great Longstone, was originally built in the eighteenth century but altered to its current neo-Tudor appearance by Mr George Marples, who purchased it in 1896 for £25,000. Here are portrayed the west front and the central hall.

163 This fine dwelling is
Bradshaw Hall, photographed in
1902. It was originally built
between 1215 and 1221 and was
then rebuilt four hundred years
later by Francis Bradshawe and
incorporates features from the
previous house, including a
staircase built in an earlier chimney
and incorporating roof timbers
from the earlier building. The Peak
has many fine old buildings built at
the beginning of the seventeenth
century, but buildings prior to this
date are unusual although some
good examples exist, such as
Haddon Hall.

Visitors

164-5 Buxton must be the oldest place in the Peak to which visitors have come, if one ignores prehistory and Arbor Low. The Romans built a bath here and for centuries a bath existed between the Old Hall Hotel and The Crescent, on the site of the Natural Baths. A pump room built by the 8th Duke of Devonshire was opened in June 1894. Here we see a rather affluent looking group of visitors taking the water. The open arches of the old Pump Room have now been filled in, thereby enlarging the building.

166 The Buxton Pavilion is a magnificent piece of Victorian iron and glass architecture, opened by the Duke of Devonshire in 1871. Although part was destroyed by fire in 1983, all of the part shown here survived. The Duke had given twelve acres of land for the purposes of creating a garden and Pavilion. Bands played in the Pavilion and bath chairs were parked outside so that their occupants could hear the music. Here they can be seen parked up side by side.

164

167 The age of the hydropathic establishment, abbreviated to 'hydro', came to Buxton as well as Matlock and other spa towns. The Palace Hotel was built in 1868 and the Empire Hotel catered for even more visitors in 1901. The latter cost £150,000 to build. This huge building seems to have been vacant after World War II until the early 1960s when it was demolished. The author can remember wandering around it as a boy, completely bewildered why such a large building could have survived unoccupied for so long. There were other hydros in Buxton — The Haddon Grove in London Road springs to mind and all seem to have been huge as many were at Matlock.

The Hot Baths, Buxton.

168-9 The baths at Buxton were situated either side of the Crescent. The Thermal or Hot Baths were at the northern end and the Natural Baths were between the Crescent and the Old Hall Hotel. Both had baths for Ladies and Gentlemen plus baths for the Buxton Bath Charity. There were public and private baths. The private hot baths (maintained at 92°F) were lined throughout with marble and these appear to have been the best. In addition to the bath itself, the hot baths offered a hot douche (similar to a hot tub or jacuzzi) plus a hot shower or vapour bath, without immersion in the water. Here are two views of the hot bath. The long corridor seems to have been a feature of both the natural and hot baths. The hot bath corridor, (shown here), was eighty feet long and the several baths were entered from this corridor. An interesting feature is the hot water pipe and radiator. The water flowed in and out of the bath and in addition, the temperature of the hot water also contributed to the moist atmosphere in the baths. In order to keep this moisture out of the rest of the building, central heating was important and very necessary to create a dry atmosphere. Both the natural baths and the hot baths were accessible from the Crescent. All the baths were drained each night and scrubbed down in order to maintain cleanliness.

The bath chairs were generally banned from the pavements around the town which is why the majority of the bath chairs on contemporary photographs are on the highway.

Thermal Mineral Water Baths, Buxton. A Corridor.

170-1 Matlock was described prior to it becoming a spa town, as a quiet hamlet in which a few framework knitters, cotton mill hands, agricultural labourers, and others, obtained a livelihood. The main reason for this was because the main road from Cromford did not then exist; the rock at Scarthin Nick, Cromford was not cut through before 1818. The town developed however during Victorian times with the establishment of around thirty hydros, many on Matlock Bank, served by a tramway up the steep Bank Road. The largest was built by John Smedley in 1853 and was substantially extended. Here are two reminders of it. The main buildings are the Winter Garden on the left-hand side plus two main blocks. The castellated part dates from around 1867 and the rest from 1885. The southern end is the old colonnade which was a covered exercise area and is now the County Library. The original buildings are on the opposite side of Smedley Street. The interior view is of the drawing room.

Smedley's Hydro closed in 1955 and is now the County Offices of Derbyshire County Council.

172 Matlock Bath Pavilion, built around 1885. It now houses an information centre and the Peak District Mining Museum, which has as its central feature a huge water-pressure pumping engine built in 1819 and recovered in 1976 from a 360ft deep lead mine near Winster.

173

175

176

173-4 The Chatsworth Hotel, Edensor, photographed around 1872 together with a close up of the hotel and some of its clients. It was built around 1775 and is a beautifully proportioned building. It was built by the Duke of Devonshire to meet the needs of travellers along his new road through Chatsworth Park. The Devonshires seem to have liked

building hostelries, for they also built the Newhaven Hotel on the Ashbourne-Buxton road and the Snake Inn on the Sheffield-Glossop road.

175-6 Derwent Hall was built in 1672 by the Balguy family and was acquired by the Derwent Valley Water Board in preparation for the construction of the Ladybower Reservoir. In 1932 it was opened as a Youth Hostel by the Prince of Wales. It was in fact, the first Youth Hostel in the Peak District, and by 1937, 27,638 people had stayed there. Initially it was the most popular Youth Hostel in the Peak District, followed by Hartington Hall which catered for 24,833 people between March 1934, when it opened, and the end of September 1937.

A minor, but none the less interesting feature of Derwent Hall was the stone carving of 'Peeping Tom' looking over the stone wall. He is the subject of a photographer's attention in the photograph of the hall and is also shown in greater detail. The carving is now preserved at Castleton Hall Youth Hostel.

177 This is Naylor's Temporance Hotel at Ecton Lea in the Manifold Valley. The field in front of the house was used as a gentleman's bowling green and a large range of greenhouses at the rear were used to grow provisions. Being situated near the Butterton Station of the Leek and Manifold Valley Light Railway it is probable that the building was first used as a hotel about the time that the railway opened in 1904 in a bid to capture some of the tourist trade. It probably ceased to be used as a hotel well before the closure of the line in 1934. The top storey of the building was removed about 1972.

178 The Market Place, Cromford. When Sir Richard Arkwright built his village for workers employed in his nearby mills, it also became necessary to cater for visitors to his mills. He therefore built the Greyhound Inn in 1778. Opposite the hotel was the blacksmith's forge which operated until 1971. Arkwright built the whole of North Street and the school at the end of it. It is situated a little way up Cromford Hill on the left.

179 A cyclist in Dovedale, negotiating The Straits. The river is in spate and the photograph was probably taken about the turn of the century.

180

180-3 We tend to take for granted areas such as Dovedale, which have been popular with tourists for centuries. Indeed, when the Natural Trust started clearing trees and scrub from the lower valley profiles of Dovedale, there was a significant local outcry. The work has exposed rock features which were previously well hidden, such as Tissington Spires and Reynards Arch. The valley is now, however, much closer to the scene that the Victorians came to see. One major exception is the exceptionally poor state of the footpath in Beresford

181

Dale, between the ford and Pike pool. In Victorian times, the footpath was hardly visible. In these four photographs we can see quite clearly how the valley used to look. The area around Pike Pool has altered, for there is now a different bridge and access to the Fishing House denied by a tall stonewall and locked doorway. The other scenes are of Reynards Cave and Arch (note the visitors at the entrance to Reynards Cave) plus Pickering Tor and Lin Dale. The donkeys were available for hire.

184 Ludchurch was as popular a venue for the Victorians as it is for today's ramblers. It has altered a little over the years. The entrance at the northern end had a white painted fence and gate which have gone. The huge landslip also had a white painted wooden statue of 'Lady Lud' perched on a ledge high above the floor. It was supposedly the figurehead from the SS *Swithamley* and features in this photograph. This ship, built in 1844, spent her life as a general trader between Liverpool and India, the East and South America. She was lost on the Blenheim reef on 1 July 1862.

184

186 Rudyard Lake near Leek was very popular with Victorian day trippers, especially after the North Staffordshire Railway built their line alongside it and constructed a station at Rudyard. Boat trips on the lake were (and still are) in demand. Here there is quite a queue for the motor launch. There are a total of twelve boats on this photograph, taken off the dam, plus a significant number of onlookers.

185 The Charles Cotton Hotel in the Market Place, Hartington, with the hotel carriage. Presumably its main use would be to carry visitors between the hotel and the railway station. The hotel was for a long time known as the Sleigh Arms. The Sleighs were a local family. The hotel had changed its name to the Charles Cotton Hotel by 1888 when a Mr Wardle was the proprietor. John Sleigh who died in 1907 and was a well known local historian, also owned Thornbridge Hall in the 1850s (see Nos 161-2). He lived there after his marriage in 1853 until 1871. For a time Mr Wardle also kept Hartington Hall as a hotel.

187 The Cat and Fiddle Inn is the
highest inn in England with a full
licence. It is conveniently situated
high on the road between Buxton
and Macclesfield and was a
convenient stopping off point for
visitors on a day trip out of the
town. Here are various cabs
patiently awaiting customers of the
inn. It was described in 1831 as
being a 'newly erected and well
accustomed inn'. The roadway
itself is an old turnpike road, said
to be the third highest in England.
Much of the original route was
superseded in the nineteenth
century and much of the original
road remains intact with its
original surface. There is a good
example of this on the Macclesfield
side of the inn where there is a
gated road leading off to the right,
or north side, of the road. This
section still has a stone milepost
giving you the mileage to London!

188   A trip to the Buxton Festival by Bradwell villagers. The photograph was possibly taken around 1910/11.

188

189

189   This is Bargate in Castleton, photographed in 1933. Castleton has long been a centre for visitors, especially with its castle, caves and Blue John stone. The stone was exploited on a bigger scale than now in Victorian times, when the veins were more plentiful. Bargate is situated on the back road to Tideswell via Little Hucklow. In the days of packhorses and horseback transport this road would probably have been much more important than it is now.

Index

The numbers in this index refer to illustrations.